Burning Bridges:
The Breakup Playbook

Ravenwolf

Copyright © 2022 by The Ravenwolf Group

All rights reserved. This book or any portion thereof may not be reproduced or used in any manner whatsoever without the express written permission of the publisher except for the use of brief quotations in a book review or the like.

First Paperback Edition: January 2022

ISBN: 979-8-88525-440-3 (print)
ISBN: 979-8-88525-441-0 (e-book)

Hyperbole Publishing
www.houseofravenwolf.com

The Breakup Playbook

Sometimes You Have to Hurt
Your Heart to Heal Your Soul 8

When You Don't Know Whether
to Wait or Forget 12

Remember Me and Smile 15

Walking Away 18

Done. Not Angry, Just Done. 21

Never Regret the Love You Gave 25

You No Longer Deserve a Reply 28

I Owe Myself an Apology for Letting
You Treat Me Like an Option 31

Sometimes It's Best to Simply Appreciate the
Time You Had Together and Move On 34

How Do You Sleep When Your Heart
and Mind Are at War? 38

Even When Someone Won't Be in the
Next Chapter ... the Story Must Go On 41

Knowing When to Let Go 45

Sometimes Strong Women
Fall in Love with Weak Men 48

How Do You Go Back to Being Strangers? 51

If You Were Lying Next to Me..................... 55

You Deserve Someone
Who Never Leaves 58

The Worst Kind of Pain 61

I May Always Miss You … but That
Doesn't Mean I'd Take You Back 64

Because That Means I'm Done 67

Too Much and Not Enough
at the Same Time 70

No Longer Losing Myself to Keep You 73

You Can Love Them
and Still Need to Leave 76

An Old Perfume, an Old Song,
an Old Memory.. 79

A Stranger Where Once
There Was a Soulmate............................... 81

Love and Pain: If One Can Fade,
So Can the Other 85

Sometimes Doing What's Right
Is the Hardest Choice................................. 89

I Didn't Quit, I Simply Chose Myself 92

Are You Aching for Me Too? 95

The Peace I Have Now
Is Worth Everything 99

My Silence Means I'm Finally Done 102

Sometimes the Purest Forum of
"I Love You" is "Goodbye" 106

When You Didn't Fight for Me 109

If It Wasn't Love, Then It Was a Lesson.. 113

The Hardest Part of Waking Up 116

I Would Rather Be Alone
Than Have a Love That Is Lonely 119

No Turning Back 122

Love Me from the Inside Out 125

I Won't Lose Who I Am
to Become What You Want 128

The Greatest Gift 131

I Never Blamed You … I Only Blamed
Me for Making You My Everything 135

Exactly Why It Had to Happen 138

You Are Strong Enough to Start Again 142

Sometimes You Have to Hurt Your Heart to Heal Your Soul

I closed my eyes and tried not to scream at the top of my lungs.

Why can't things just work out the way I want them to?

I had come to learn through so much frustration that, sometimes, we don't get what we ask for ... because we get what we need instead.

I knew that he was bad for me in every way, toxic even, but I was just so drawn to him when I shouldn't have been ...

But I had to break free if I was ever going to reclaim my self-respect and peace.

Many years from now, I knew that I would look back at this defining moment and realize that I made the right choice ...

But those hard decisions just hurt so much in the moment ... the right now can be so hard.

You can't breathe, the walls seem to close in around you and the world just seems so dark.

Why must I say goodbye to someone that I love?

Because sometimes, people need to stay in your heart, but not your life.

He had led me down a terrible road and caused me so much pain, yet for some reason, I hadn't been able to let go ... until now.

It hurt worse than anything I've ever known, but trying to love a toxic person slowly eats away at everything you are ...

And I just couldn't do it anymore.

I had lost pieces of myself trying to fix him, and I was just tired.

I needed more than rest; I needed a change ...

And I had to get away from the person I once thought was my everything to have the kind of future I knew I deserved.

He may never understand and might even hate me for it, but that's okay ...

I'm doing what's best for both of us.

It won't be easy, and there will be many times I'll want to pick up the phone and reach out to him ... but I can't, I won't.

My story had turned into a tale of anger, jealousy and rage from a person who said they loved me, and I couldn't live like that anymore.

That isn't who I'm meant to be – I'm capable of becoming so much more.

They say doing the right thing will set you free, but the truth is that it will break you first.

It shattered me and my heart into a million pieces as I trudged through each day trying not to think, not to feel ...

But this is what I know – I have to be broken, beautifully so, to let the light into my soul to chase out the darkness.

I've dwelled so long in misery that sometimes I don't even know how to find the light on my own ...

So, these steps I take now are for my heart, my future and to let the light in again.

I don't know which way I'm headed or how I'll make it through the day sometimes, but I'll get stronger as each day passes.

It's not easy as I cry in the shower and lay in bed awake at night, but it's necessary to move on, to grow.

This will not define me, this pain and heartache.

My story will be one of triumph and rising from the ashes.

He pushed me to the edge, but now I can see the truth of what he and I became … and it wasn't healthy.

I'll lose myself in my friends, my music and my hope, because that's how I'll keep getting stronger.

One day, it'll stop hurting and the painful memories will begin fading away.

Until then, I'll keep my face to the light, surround myself with those who feel like sunshine and always remember that brighter days are ahead.

Like always, I can do it ...

I got this.

When You Don't Know Whether to Wait or Forget

I lie in bed, wide awake –
I can't sleep because I can't shut off my thoughts.
I'm in that weird place that doesn't allow my mind to stop ...
The thoughts, the cares and concerns, just keep turning over in my mind.
My heart and my head are waging war and I'm caught in the middle.
It's the most difficult place to be when you don't know what to do.
My head tells me to walk away, that you'll never figure out what you want,
And why wait forever when that's how long it might take you to know if you want to make this work ...
Or if you even love me.
My heart tells me to hang on, give you the space and time to sort out your feelings.
That we could have something beautiful once we get past this weird place that we're in.

It makes my heart hurt a little more every day as we linger ...

I don't know if I should move on and try to forget you ... or if I should hold and hope this works out.

They say love isn't enough, and I'm holding my breath hoping that you'll discover what I mean to you ...

I've loved you for longer than I care to admit, and truthfully, parts of me wish I hadn't fallen for you.

But there's no going back.

I'm at a crossroads that makes me cry in the shower as I just want so much for us to work out ... but we're in limbo because you say you just don't know.

You can want someone so much that it hurts physically, and there's times that I can't breathe as I think of losing you.

But as the night falls and I'm lost in a montage of happy thoughts of us,

I would give anything to just stop thinking.

Until the realization of how empty this feels slowly dawns on me, and I finally know:

I can't do this anymore.

It's tearing me apart, and if you don't care, don't want this or can't "figure it out," I'm moving on.

My self-respect, my self love and my happiness are worth more than staying in limbo hoping you'll decide you want me.

The sun will rise tomorrow on a different me with a different plan …

And I'm going to hold firm and do what I know I must:

Walk away.

Not because I don't care or I don't love you, but because you don't.

I'm tired of the sleepless night and tears.

I gave you all the chances and did everything I could to make this work.

It takes two, and you're just not here with me …

You may never get here.

And I won't be here anymore to find out.

I loved you the best I could, but I finally understand …

Sometimes, love alone just isn't enough.

Remember Me and Smile

I was scrolling through my phone today, and I came across a picture of us.

It startled me – I didn't expect to see that memory, and it caught me off guard.

I thought I had deleted all of those pictures long ago, and with good reason … I no longer allow baggage to weigh me down.

It was one of those moments when you could see the happiness in our faces and the sparkle in our eyes.

I put the phone down, and my mind began to race with memories of a time long ago …

When we were young, love was new, and the world seemed full of endless possibilities.

The adventurous fun, the spontaneous laughter and the soul-filled love we shared seemed like it would never end.

We lived to the fullest and loved like every day was our last.

Truthfully, I can't tell you why we didn't make it, but it's been so long, it doesn't really matter anyway.

I made peace with our past long ago, so I can hold onto the beautiful memories that make me smile.

I've long since let go of all the negative stuff, because all it ever did was weigh me down.

Once upon a time, I cried countless tears and endured so many sleepless nights because of us ...

I'm past that now.

So, I choose to remember the happiness we had, the love we shared and the life we enjoyed together.

It doesn't make me sad anymore – I wish you nothing but the best in your life.

I've moved on, and I'm sure you have too.

I smile as the thoughts of a time long past flood my mind.

For a time, it was beautiful, it was love and it was us.

That will always be what I remember about you ... because that's what makes me happy.

Maybe we weren't meant to be.

And you're just a memory now anyway.

But I choose to remember the good things, because happiness is and always will be a much better place for me to be.

Some people were meant to be in your heart, not in your life.

Walking Away

You thought that I'd always be there for you, no matter how you treated me ...

But I deserve better than what you've given me.

I don't know how or why our relationship changed, but somewhere along the way it turned dark and ugly.

Our beautiful love story slowly transformed into something completely different ...

And it breaks my heart a little more each day.

I don't know why you ever started to disrespect and disregard my feelings, but it tears me apart when you do.

I've tried to talk to you, I've done everything I know to do, and it doesn't seem to matter to you.

Somewhere along the way you became angry and resentful, and I don't understand why ...

But maybe I never will.

Truthfully, maybe you were always the person I see in front of me right now, and I just didn't see it before ... a person can only wear a mask for so long, you know.

You fooled me and my heart – I felt stupid at first, but now I realize maybe you don't even know who you are.

It doesn't matter anymore ...

I've decided I have to stop trying to make us work and make myself happy instead.

Your hurtful words and diminishing actions, I never deserved any of that ... no one does.

For a moment, you almost made me stopped believing in myself ... but I'm stronger than that.

I'm done living my life holding my breath waiting for the next disaster or angry outburst.

I'm standing up for myself and walking away from you.

I hope you find what you need someday, because I know you have a beautiful heart underneath all the ugliness, but I'm not going to be there to find out.

I know who I am and what I'm worth, something I don't think you've seen for a long time ... if ever.

The next few days and months will be hard, and I know there will be a lot of times I won't be able to stop crying, but I have to take care of me now.

I've been trying to fix you for too long, and it's almost broken me in the process.

Truthfully, I don't know where I'm going or what tomorrow may bring, but this is a journey I must take to reclaim the parts of me that I lost in us.

I know you won't understand and that's fine … I don't expect you to.

It'll be my fault and you'll blame me for everything … I accept that, sadly.

Not because it's true, but because we both know it's not.

Thank you for showing me love for a time and most of all, helping me to see what I don't want in a relationship.

For a time, it was beautiful, it was love and it was us …

But I'm going to stop hoping for the impossible change in you and start living for myself again.

It won't be easy, it won't be painless,

But at least I'll be happy on my own terms.

For now, that's all I can ask for.

Done. Not Angry, Just Done.

She had finally reached that point ... where feelings didn't matter, and she no longer cared.

She had fought so long and so hard to save her relationship, she was more than tired ...

Her soul was weary.

She couldn't pour any more into the hope of working things out and finding a way to stay together.

She didn't know why he had changed or had stopped loving her the way she knew she deserved, but it was obvious to her that he had.

He would deny it and shrug off her concerns, but her intuition told her a different story.

She couldn't remember why things had slowly disintegrated between them, only that she felt farther away from him with each passing day.

In fact, she felt like she was the only one who cared about them ... he would say he did, but his actions never backed up his words.

She had finally gotten to the point where her heart had given up.

She wasn't mad, upset or crying anymore ...

She was just done.

The pain was slowly going away, and it was being replaced by numbness.

She couldn't fight any more for someone who wasn't willing to fight for her.

She deserved better, and if he wouldn't step up, then she needed to move on ...

And everything she saw, knew and felt just reinforced that it was that time to seek happiness elsewhere, away from him.

She had already spent countless nights crying and even more times trying to talk to him, but he refused to communicate.

All he did was get angry when she tried to reach out to him to work through their challenges.

No more.

She was done being verbally abused, put down and taken for granted.

It saddened her that she couldn't even remember why they loved each other anymore ... She was simply surviving, and that's no way to live.

She had a choice – either fight for someone who didn't care or move on and find her own happiness.

So, she made the hard choice and walked away …

And he only made it easier with his nonchalance and lack of concern.

She wasn't turning her back on him, she was turning to face the light of hope and happiness again.

It had been so long since she'd been truly happy, her tired heart welcomed the change like a breath of fresh air.

She knew it would hurt for a while, but in the end, she valued her self-respect, herself and her happiness most of all.

Maybe he'd never really see it, but she knew she was worth it ...

In fact, she deserved so much more than he ever gave her.

Now, she was finally done with him and opening her heart to new possibilities ...

And with that,

She broke free of the cage he had tried to keep her in.

Finally, she was free to live, to love and most of all, to be happy in the ways she'd always wanted.

Never Regret the Love You Gave

As I look back and try to figure out what happened between us, a flurry of images and memories of us cross my mind.

I think about our time together and try to remember the good things instead of what went wrong.

It doesn't do me any good to start thinking about why we fell apart, because I can't go back and change what happened.

It still hurts, but a little less every day.

I'm not bitter about us parting ways, I only wish that we hadn't been so angry at the end.

We were never meant to be, and I know that now.

No amount of wishing and hoping can change the past, so I've learned to let go a little more every day.

Each day I wake up I find that I think of you less and the pain subsides a bit more.

Once, all I could think of was you and our life together – our plans, our hopes and our dreams.

That's what made me happy and believe that anything was possible.

But I've learned that our paths sometimes don't go as we'd hoped, and I've made peace with that.

I close my eyes each morning, take a deep breath and remind myself that when one door closes, another opens ... a better opportunity that life has in store for me.

It's not always easy to look forward, the past seems to constantly be tugging at my heart.

I've finally realized, though, that I'll never regret the time we had and the love we shared ...

At one time, it was exactly what I wanted and made me so very happy.

Perhaps things didn't go as planned and we are on different journeys now, but I don't regret a moment I spent loving you.

Because of you, I learned so much about myself, and I wouldn't change that for anything.

I'm stronger, wiser and braver because of you.

So, as I wish you the best in life, know that I'll always care about you, no matter where your path takes you.

Thank you for loving me for a time and for the memories we made ...

But most of all, thank you for helping me find myself again, reawakening the person I had lost along the way.

You No Longer Deserve a Reply

Once, I would have clung to your every word and wanted nothing more than to be close to you.

Now, times have changed and the pain I once felt as you walked away from me is gone.

The stinging hurt has been replaced by something very different ... numbness.

I wish things had gone differently between us, but I've since realized that things happen the way they are meant to ...

We were never going to be forever, and as hard as it was, making peace with that helped me see why I needed to focus on myself.

The pain of your loss felt so heavy that I was overwhelmed with the hurt that permeated my entire being.

Now, you're a memory that elicits mixed feelings of regret and relief.

So, as I see your words pop up on my phone, I'm startled for a moment, seeing a blast from the past.

A myriad of emotions washes over me as the memories come flooding back ...

But the pain that once would have made me cry just doesn't come ...

I'm where I always needed to be.

I'm done.

I'm over you.

It's been a hard road and a lot of sleepless nights, but I made it through the darkness to find myself once again.

I'll never forget what we once had and the love we shared, but that all seems like a lifetime ago ... a faded memory of another me.

I'm stronger because of you, and I have to thank you for who you forced me to become ...

I'm better, wiser, and I love myself more than I ever did.

So, I smile wistfully as I see your words ...

How am I doing?

Oh, my dear, I'm doing great.

As I click "delete," I beam with satisfaction.

I'm awesome ... and that's all you'll never need to know.

You missed your chance with me, and I'm not looking back ...

My future is too bright to wait around for someone who doesn't understand just how amazing I am.

That's okay ... I know, and in the end, that's what really matters most.

I Owe Myself an Apology for Letting You Treat Me Like an Option

I tried to tell myself that you loved me the best way you knew how, but I was just lying to myself.

I let you treat me in a way that I never should have allowed, and it's my fault for letting that happen.

I'm not going to blame you for being who you are, that's just your nature.

I'm better than that, but for some reason, I forgot that when we met.

I stopped standing up for myself and letting my voice be heard.

I don't know why I ever accepting being just an option when I always should have been a priority.

Truth is, it took a lot of tears and sleepless nights to make me realize that the only way I could be happy with you was to walk away.

I let you get comfortable treating me in ways so much less than I deserve, and I'm leaving because I have more self-respect than to keep chasing the affection of someone who's unwilling to give it as they should.

I shouldn't have to fight for your attention or beg for you to spend time with me ... those are things you should have just wanted to do because you loved me.

I don't know if you'll ever change or if you'll just find someone willing to be okay with being second best, but that's not me nor will it ever be again.

I have to thank you for waking me up and reminding me never to settle for anyone or anything less than the best.

I know my worth and what I deserve, and you never saw that in me ...

Which makes me sad, mostly for you.

We could have had an amazing love story, but your ego and inability to change will be a testament to your selfish style of love ...

And I don't want that in my life, now or ever.

I'm walking away, shaking my head at my foolishness but stronger because I refused to be treated that way and made the hard choice.

I'm taking back my power and keeping my standards and hopes high.

I know who I am and what I deserve, but I learned a lot from you ... mostly what I don't want in a partner.

I wish you the best in your life, but the lessons you taught me will last me a lifetime ...

I'm sorry for my part in the fights, the bad feelings and hurt emotions, but most of all,

I owe myself the biggest apology for allowing you to treat me poorly.

You showed everything I don't want, and now, I'm aiming for the stars.

I'm not holding out for a hero, I'm the hero of my own tale ...

and come what may, I'll find my love story ...

This time, it'll be real, it'll be respectful, and it will be forever ...

Just the way I've always deserved.

Sometimes It's Best to Simply Appreciate the Time You Had Together and Move On

As I turned and watched you walk away, I fought the tears back as the memories of us flashed through my mind.

The good times and the bad, the joy and the pain, the love and the laughter … I saw it all.

It made me sad and happy at the same time, and my heart felt like it could explode.

I now know that sometimes, you have to cherish the good memories and let the bad stuff go …

I want to remember us and smile, because all the bad things won't do me any good to keep reliving …

So, I'm banishing those bad moments and thoughts because I don't need them anymore … and I'm going to hang onto the bits of happiness we once had,

Not the sadness that our pain will bring back.

I don't know how we got to this place, where we lost our way from the love that was once so amazing.

We celebrated the good times and stood together during the hard days, but in the end, what we had just wasn't meant to be.

I'll always love you and you'll forever have a place in my heart, but as they say, sometimes love just isn't enough.

We could never communicate through the hardships the way we both wanted to – almost as if we spoke different languages at times.

You'd wall yourself off from me and we just couldn't talk – maybe you just didn't want to.

I did my fair share of things wrong, too, I know that now.

We can't go back and change the way things happened, undo the fights and hurt feelings, and I know now it's for the best.

It hurts in a way that I've never felt, but that's how you know you really care about someone.

I wish sometimes, I could just turn off my heart ... but I can't.

I won't.

We made the best of a passionate love that was never meant to be, and we hung on for too long to a story that was always going to end.

We loved, we fought, we tried, and we failed ...

But we never stopped loving, no matter how hard it got.

So, as you disappear from my sight, tears stream down my face for the memories we made together.

I can't imagine my life without you, but now, I'll have to do just that.

I'll probably bawl when I hear our favorite song and sigh when something reminds me of you, but life will be different now, and I just have to accept that.

Maybe we will meet again someday, and things will be different, but I won't let myself think about that.

For now, I'm going to smile about the memories, laugh about the joy we had and celebrate a love that once was ...

My days will be strange without you in them, but this is the road I must take now.

I'm going to rediscover myself and what makes me happy.

This is my time to dig deep and find my joy in all the places I stopped looking because of us.

I owe that to myself, and more than that, I owe it to my heart and my future.

I don't have the answers, and I may never figure them all out, but all I can do is very simple ...

Keep my face to the sunlight and live in the moments of my life.

That, for now, will have to be enough.

One day at a time, I'll find my way back to where I'm meant to be, I know that now ...

I'll find the happiness I once lost along the way to my dreams.

I just didn't know where to look before ...

Sometimes, the most beautiful joys can come out of the worst things if you know how to let go of the pain ...

This time, I'm going to open my heart, free my mind and forever seek the light.

How Do You Sleep When Your Heart and Mind Are at War?

I try to do whatever I can to quiet my thoughts, but often, nothing works.

The television, music … anything I can find to drown out the deafening noise of my mind.

I tell myself that everything will work out the way it's supposed to, but my heart won't rest, and my thoughts never quit.

I replay where I've been and what's happened, the turns and twists of our relationship, and still, I lie there and stare at the ceiling …

Consumed by the relentless overthinking that is my way.

I can't remember a time when I could turn off my mind, and I've come to accept that's just who I am …

But when my heart battles my mind at night, it can become almost overwhelming.

My head tells me to let it go, make peace with the broken road I've traveled, but my heart won't let me.

It tells me to keep fighting, to hold on, that loving someone means struggling and making it through the hard times together.

I can't help but cry in these times when everything inside me is at war with what I should do.

The tears flow as I fight to regain my composure, but it's impossible sometimes to keep it together.

Maybe when I get up tomorrow I'll feel better or have some ideas about what I should do, but right now, I just feel utterly lost.

Conflict wages inside every corner of me, with no end in sight.

I just want ... peace.

I close my eyes and think back to simpler times when love was new and hope was fresh.

I find myself slowly drifting off as those warm thoughts wrap around me like a comforting blanket, giving me much-needed peace.

As my heart and mind slow, my dreams whisk me away to a more serene place, and my last thought before succumbing to exhaustion is but a simple wish ...

Maybe tomorrow, somehow, I'll find my way to a happier place … and there,

I'll remember what it means to be content again … where my mind and heart can finally agree with what's best for me.

Until then, I'll just do what I can with what I have …

And the simple reminder that gives me solace if but for a moment as I drift off:

It's always darkest before dawn.

I know that tomorrow will have to be a better day …

If not, I'll just keep pushing forward and hope for moments of quiet midst my thoughts.

For me, for now, that will have to be enough.

Even When Someone Won't Be in the Next Chapter … the Story Must Go On

As I turned and walked away, I felt the tears welling up in my eyes.

The memories of what we had and the love we once shared flashed through my mind in a long-since gone montage of happiness.

It's easy to remember the good stuff when you're thinking about someone –

My soul couldn't take reliving the heartache and pain that we had endured as a couple.

The bitterness and angst that made me cry so many nights … I simply didn't want to feel that again.

I looked back over my shoulder one last time at you, seeing you standing there, motionless as I walked away.

I could see your pain, eyes watering, and it hurt me deeply – maybe one of the hardest things I've ever had to do was walk away from you.

But it was something that I had to do for us both to find happiness again.

We both knew that we couldn't make us work, no matter how hard we tried or how much we loved.

Sometimes, love just isn't enough.

You travel down a broken road so long with someone that sometimes you forget what you're fighting for.

The why and the love gets replaced by trying to find a middle ground ...

You stop seeing the joy and beauty of your love and just try not to suffocate under the weight of anguish.

And that's never going to be enough for me – and it shouldn't be enough for you, either.

I smiled one last time as I turned a corner and saw you for the last time.

Those powerful moments can be overwhelming, but they're also a lesson of growth ...

Time slows to almost a standstill as your eyes meet for one last time ...

And then, it's like they were never there ...
such an important part of your life ... vanished.

We weren't ever meant to be and continuing to hold onto a broken relationship was making us both miserable.

In the end, saying goodbye to you and to us was one the hardest things I've ever had to do, but I know it's for the best.

I'll always love and care about you, that will never change.

Some people were meant to be in your heart, not your life.

So, as I close the chapter of our life and love, a solitary tear rolls down my cheek.

I'll never forget what you meant to me and the times we shared.

I'm making the hard decision to walk away to find real and lasting love ...

Most of all, for myself ... I had lost that part of me for so long with you.

Now, I'm taking my power back and forging a new path,

But I'll never forget you and the love we had.

For a time, it was us, it was beautiful, and it was love.

That'll always be how I remember it.

Here's to new chapters and happy endings ...

Sometimes, you just have to know when to make new memories and let the old stuff go.

Maybe the next door that opens will be different ... that's all I can hope for.

That, and for you to be happy ...

Such is the way our stories go sometimes.

Knowing When to Let Go

Deep down, part of me knew that you really didn't ever love me the way I deserved.

I lied to myself for so long, trying to convince myself that this was it, that our love was the one I had always searched for.

I sacrificed so much of who I was as I tried to make our love into something that it was never meant to be.

I think you tried to love me in the best way you knew how, but I know now that was never going to be enough for me ...

Your love was never going to be enough.

I pretended that I was okay fighting for your attention, but the truth was, I could never accept being just an option for you.

So, I forgive you as I walk away, knowing that you never meant to hurt me.

It's my fault for not loving myself enough to stop settling and to start fighting for what I deserve ...

So that's what I'm doing now.

I'm standing up, I'm speaking up ... stating my mind and starting to reclaim my faded soul.

I realize that you're not part of my happily ever after, and that's okay.

You're the chapter that pushed me to remember who I am and what I want.

I had to be truly lost to know that I needed to start looking for myself again.

You taught me so much about myself that I couldn't have learned any other way.

You've helped me rediscover the parts of myself that I lost along the way.

I'm taking back my power and setting my heart on fire.

I know what I want and what I need, and I'm never again going to accept anything less.

I don't need to be perfect or for my life to be easy to find happiness,

But I do need to be loved for who I am the way I deserve ...

I will wait for the one who will see past my eyes into my soul and who will know my worth.

I'm not holding out for a hero; I'm saving myself the best way I know how.

By loving myself in the way I always should have ...

And letting the rest take care of itself.

Some things are worth fighting for,
Most of all … me.

Sometimes Strong Women Fall in Love with Weak Men

When I saw you across the street,
I found myself smiling.
The kind of grin that is thoughtful and wistful.
Not because I miss you or I'd change anything about the life we once shared,
But because we will always have those wonderful memories of a love that was never meant to be.
We don't always choose who we fall in love with, but the chapters we write are up to us … mostly.
No matter how deeply we loved or the promises we made, I learned it takes much more than love to last forever.
Maybe it's written in the stars, maybe our hearts know the truth all along, or maybe destiny holds the cards of who makes it and who doesn't.
I don't blame you for what happened, really, because you loved me the best way you knew how …

But my spirit was too fierce and my passion too intense for us to ever really have had a chance.

You gave our love everything you had, but deep down, we both know you didn't truly understand my soul the way I needed.

You said you wanted a brave and strong woman, that you needed passion in your life ... but along the way, the very things that drew you to me just pushed you away.

I wasn't ever meant to be tamed, controlled or watered down ...

You finally realized that I wouldn't ever be the woman you thought you needed all along.

In letting me go, though, you thought you broke my heart ...

But really you set me free.

To find who I really was and have the chance to meet someone else that loved and appreciated me just the way I am ...

Unconditionally.

So, as I see you across the way, my smile brightens as I think back to the times we had.

You helped me become the person that I was meant to be, all along.

Thank you for loving and caring about me –
you'll always have a place in my heart.
Most of all, you showed me that some people were meant to be in your heart,
Not in your life.
Thank you for setting me free ... to fly high like I was always meant to ...
Happy, strong and free.

How Do You Go Back to Being Strangers?

I thought I could just forget you ...

That the pain of losing you wouldn't hurt so badly ...

But I was wrong.

I wanted to bury the feelings we once shared in a place where they wouldn't cut me anymore ...

But that's impossible.

I knew I'd never truly heal if I didn't face my pain.

Of all the things you told me, I just can't forget how you said you would always be there.

Promises of loyalty have now faded away to forgotten words.

You made it seem easy when you walked away, like what we had just didn't matter ...

But it does.

It always will.

I can't just forget someone who meant so very much to me like they didn't even exist,

Even if you can, I can't and won't.

I'll always cherish what we had, because it was beautiful in its time, in its way.

I learned so much from you and because of you, I'd never change anything.

I forgive you for the anguish you caused, because I'm better than holding onto the past, No matter how painful.

Dwelling on what happened between us and over-analyzing what went wrong didn't do anything for me but cause me sleepless nights and countless tears.

Truth is, I'll never really know why you quit on us or how you could turn your back on me so easily.

I've had to make peace with the fact that you were never meant to be my person, and though it hurt so badly, it's gotten better as the days have passed.

There were many days when I didn't want to get out of bed, and I ignored everyone's calls.

I couldn't see the light for the darkness I tried to blame on you ...

That's when I woke up and realized you couldn't help the way you were, and we can't change what's meant to be.

People come into your life for a season, a reason or a lesson … and you were all three for me.

You made me remember how strong I was before you, no matter how hard the challenges life threw at me.

As I look at your picture on my phone, a sad wistful smile creeps into the corners of my mouth … because I know I should thank you …

For setting me free, for reminding me of who I am,

And most of all, forcing me to find a way through the pain of heartbreak.

I'm stronger now than I've ever been.

It may be some time before it gets easier, but every day that passes, I get a little stronger …

A little wiser.

A little happier.

It's strange thinking that later in my life, I'll look back and you'll be just another person that passed through, a chapter that closed ever so painfully …

But that's the thing about my story.

It's just getting started, and I've got sparkle in my eyes again.

My soul is remembering how to be alive once more.

This time, I'm taking the pen and writing my story just how I should have all along.

With passionate love, soulful life and unbreakable purpose.

I'm doing it all my way ...

Because now,

More than ever ...

I'm beautiful, I'm strong and I'll always be unbreakable.

If You Were Lying Next to Me

There are those times at night when I look over at the empty place in the bed beside me and try not to cry.

I fight back the tears because I can't let the dam break … or I'll be crying for hours.

Maybe it's loneliness, maybe I miss you,

Or maybe it's a little bit of both.

Truthfully, I don't really know.

All I do know is that my thoughts run wild with the flashes of the memories we made together and the love we shared.

I always knew that nothing is forever, but I wish so very much you were lying beside me ...

Breathing as you slept, peacefully quiet as the serenity of night enveloped us in a protective cocoon.

I'd snuggle up to you and smile as your eyes would open –

The corners of your mouth would curl into that smirking smile I so adored, and I'd lean in and kiss you.

You'd wistfully ask me why I was awake, and I would try not to blurt out every random thought had crossed my mind for the last few hours ...

I'd smile warmly and just say, "you know, stuff on my mind."

Those are the memories that come creeping back in the middle of the night as I am missing you.

The talks we had, the laughs and love we shared and the life we faced together.

It wasn't perfect, but it always seemed to work for us in its own special way.

So, as a solitary tear rolls down my cheek, I force a smile through the storms of my discontent.

Those are the times I cling to – the happiness that we had – and somehow, it gets me through.

It may never be fully enough, but it helps me survive the hard moments ... when do you ever get enough of the right kind of love?

I curl into a ball and close my eyes, remembering that this too, shall pass.

Sleep overwhelms me as a bittersweet thought sweeps over me:

For a time, it was us, it was beautiful, and it was love.

You Deserve Someone Who Never Leaves

What hurt me most isn't that we fought and you said hurtful things.
I'm thick-skinned and I can get past words ... though words can cut the deepest.
What breaks my heart is that instead of fighting for us and working with me to find a way through our problems,
You chose to walk away and turn your back on me.
You took the easy way out, and now that you've decided you're ready to come back,
You think that I should be welcoming you with open arms?
Truth is, I can't just bury the pain between us and the hurt you caused when you ran.
You think I should be grateful you came back?
Think again, my dear.
I may have been broken, and I may not always know the right answers, but I do know this:
I know who I am and what I'm worth ...
More than that, I know what I deserve.

You've always seemed to think that you know what's best for me, but you proved otherwise when you hurt me by leaving.

I don't need to be rescued or fixed, and I don't need anyone to make me happy ...

There's a big difference between want and need ...

And what I need most in a partner is courage ... someone who won't walk out on me when things get hard ...

A partner who will be a rock through the storms when we need it most.

I used to think that was you, and I'm sad now that I've realized it's not.

Thank you for loving me in your way and for helping me to understand what I truly deserve in life and love ...

And it's not someone who can't handle the hard stuff, a partner who quits when the going gets tough.

I'll never need anyone to be happy with myself, so I've decided next time,

I'm not settling for just anyone to love me,

I'm holding out for a hero.

Because that's who I am and exactly what I deserve.

It doesn't take heroism to believe in love,

But it does take someone who will do the one thing you couldn't ...

fight for us, each and every day.

The Worst Kind of Pain

What hurts the most as I think about hearing those painful words you said isn't what you said ... but who said them.

When our love was young and new you told me you'd never forsake me.

You promised me that you'd never leave me and that you would stand beside me through any storm.

I'd been hurt so many times before, and though I didn't trust love,

You made me believe I could trust you enough to take my walls down.

That you'd not break my heart like the ones before.

I wanted to let you in to see the real me, to finally have someone who saw and loved me for me.

But in those few seconds when you turned your back on me, everything that we had built – and once believed in – came crashing down.

I never thought you'd be the one to break my heart because you knew the journey I'd taken to heal.

You knew how scared I was to love again, and still you decided to go instead of staying and trying to save us.

I can forgive you for so much, but never for leaving and giving up without fighting for love, for us.

There were no words that could comfort my ailing spirit and no light behind my eyes, for our once beautiful future had fallen into decay.

As I watched you walk away, I fought back the tears and struggled to keep it together.

Some people come into your life for a season, a reason or a lesson ...

You were all those things for me when I most needed to find a way to believe again.

In love, in hope ...

That maybe dreams can come true.

Yes, it hurt for a long time when you left – I may never truly get over you ...

But I know as more time passes, I will be grateful for you and what you taught me.

It doesn't mean it will be easy to accept or the memories won't be painful,

But I'll realize the truth of what you showed me.

It's okay to open your heart and believe in love even when some people may not deserve or appreciate that love.

It's up to us to figure out who truly is worth it.

While you weren't the one meant to be my person, you did show me the way to a healthier and happier me.

I guess I should thank you midst my tears for setting me free.

Somewhere, someone else is looking for a love like mine.

That, for now, will be more than enough to make me smile ...

And find a way to believe again.

I May Always Miss You … but That Doesn't Mean I'd Take You Back

I came across a picture of you the other day and I couldn't help but smile.

Not because seeing you made me happy, but because I will always have the memories ...

Some good, some bad ... all very real.

The times we had and the love we shared will always have a special place in my heart.

We fought for a love that just wasn't meant to be – but it doesn't change how I'll always feel about you.

You can love someone and know that they belong in your heart, not your life.

Truth is, I can't really remember why we didn't make it, and it doesn't matter now.

I won't think poorly of you or of us, because we had something beautiful for a time.

You loved me in your way and tried your best to always make me feel special ...

I'll forever appreciate that about you.

I learned so much about life and love from my time with you, and I wouldn't change a thing, even if I could.

Love sometimes isn't enough to carry two people past the emotional distress they face together.

You need more than that: respect, empathy, compassion and communication.

I'll never forget you and the magical kisses and frozen moments in time that will always have a special place in my heart.

A tiny part of me will forever miss you and wish we were together again, but I know things happen for a reason ...

I'm happier now for what happened and what I learned after we parted ways.

We were never meant to find our forever together, and though I cried endless tears many nights about losing you, I know now that I'm a better person because of what happened between us.

You forced me to look harder at the parts of myself that I tried to bury in our relationship –

I can't thank you enough for helping me to understand the path to a happier and healthier me.

So, if I ever saw you somewhere across the way, I'd look at you and simply smile at the memories of what we once had.

For a time

It was real, it was beautiful and it was love.

But I'll always be glad you let me go ...

That's when I finally learned how to truly love myself.

Because That Means I'm Done

I told you before that if we ever got to a point where I stopped caring, I would be done.

Not fighting, crying or being angry ...

No reconciliation, no working through things ... just done.

Because slowly, with every fight, each night spent crying and the passing of angry words between us, a little more of my love for you died.

I wish I didn't feel this way, but I can't help what heart tells me is true.

I'm not mad or emotional about us anymore ...

I'm just numb, and that's the worst place to be.

I can't bring back what was there before, and I can't make my heart feel differently.

I'm just not there anymore.

I'm not in love with you now, not like I was ... and I won't ever be again.

I'm not doing this to hurt you, I'm giving you the respect you deserve and being honest with you.

I will always love you, and you'll always have a special place in my heart, but when I'm done ...

I'm just done.

There's no coming back from this ...

And I know it hurts you, but I can't live a lie.

We've come too far, and my heart whispers what my head already knew.

I can't manufacture love, and I can't promise you something that is gone ... and those feelings I had aren't there anymore.

We tried to make this love into forever, but we were never meant to be.

Some people come into your life for a season, a reason or a lifetime, and there's so much I've learned from you.

So, I'll never regret us, for I learned ...

What I don't want in a life or love story ...

And most of all, what I'm willing to accept.

I deserve to be a priority, and you never really thought I was important enough for that.

So, while it hurts to look at you with tears streaming down your face, I know it's the right decision: it's time to find our own ways on different paths ...

We were never meant to be forever.

You'll find someone someday who loves you how you want to be loved, but it won't be me.

I'll look back on this time and smile at our memories while continuing forward.

That, for me, will be enough.

So, I'm saying goodbye to us so I can say hello to a new me, a happier me.

Losing someone and moving on is always a little sad, but I know it's for the best –

For both of us.

I hope one day you'll understand why I feel the way I do.

That you'll come to see that what I did I did for both of us ...

Because you deserve to be happy too –

And you never would have found that with me.

Too Much and Not Enough at the Same Time

I tried so hard to be what you wanted, and it just wasn't enough.

I gave you my heart, and I thought we would be forever …

But I was wrong.

I don't know if you just fell out of love with me or never really loved me at all ...

And I may never know the truth.

You told me all the reasons why you we're walking away, and all I could do was cry ...

Partly because I didn't understand and partly because I deserved better.

I did everything, gave you everything, but it wasn't enough ...

Which is one of the hardest feelings to experience – not being enough.

Apparently, I was too much of the things you didn't like and not enough of the things you wanted ...

Which breaks my heart.

I'm going to move on after a lot of tears and probably a few sleepless nights, even though deep down I know this is for the best …

I just wish I could convince my heart of that.

I would never have been what you wanted, no matter how much I tried to change ...

Which really isn't love at all.

Unconditional real love is accepting and appreciating someone just the way they are.

I've learned from you the most valuable lesson of all:

You can't change to make someone love you, because you'll end up not liking the person you've become.

I lost parts of myself trying to be what you said you wanted, and I'm never doing that again.

If someone can't love me for who I am, then they don't deserve me.

I'm done lowering my standards and accepting a love that isn't true.

Maybe I'll end up alone, maybe I'll have to wait a long time, maybe love will find me tomorrow … but at least I'll make my journey through life the way that makes me truly happy …

Being who I am instead of what someone else thinks I should be.

After all, my happiness is what matters most.

Love on my terms or not at all, that's my choice from now on.

Because of you, I'm finally free to find myself, my love and my truths ...

Just the way I've always wanted.

No Longer Losing Myself to Keep You

You always said you loved me for who I was, that you wouldn't change a thing.

We both know that wasn't true.

There were little signs along the way that I chose to ignore, hoping that they didn't really mean anything.

How wrong I was.

You didn't want me for the person I was, you wanted me to change into what you thought you wanted ...

And truthfully, I don't think you had any idea what that was, maybe you never will.

In fact, you don't need a partner, you want someone to do for you what you won't do for yourself.

You would never admit it, but you want someone to worship you, do whatever you ask and then love you as well.

I don't want a project; I want a partner.

I'm not going to be your lover, your maid, your mother and your moneymaker.

That's not fair to anyone, and that's why I'm walking away now.

I know you'll try to tell me that you'll change, but that's a broken record I've heard too many times before.

I've already lost too much of myself trying to love you, and I'm done sacrificing my dreams and desires to make you happy ...

Because you won't ever be content.

I don't even know if you truly know what it means to love someone the right way – in all the ways that matter,

Not according to what they can do for you.

A relationship is supposed to be a give and take, but I don't think you got the memo,

Because while you've got the taking part down, you don't have a clue how to give ...

And I'm done trying to ask for your affection, attention and love.

I should never have to fight for that.

So, I wish you the best in wherever life takes you, just know that I won't be waiting for you anymore at the end of your days hoping you'll love me the way I deserve.

This will hurt and it will be hard, but even the thought of leaving feels like a burden has been lifted – and that's how I know I'm doing the right thing.

I'll always love you and keep the happy memories in my heart, but I'm choosing now to take back my life and find myself again.

I deserve the kind of love that is unconditionally beautiful and loyally unselfish ...

And instead of asking anyone else to do that for me ...

I'm going to love myself the way I should have all along.

It won't be easy, it won't be fast, but it will all be worth it in the end.

So, I'm taking the first steps on my journey back to who I'm meant to be ...

Freedom never felt as wonderful as it does right now.

You Can Love Them and Still Need to Leave

She sat down and buried her face in her hands, fighting back tears, because she knew what she had to do ...

And it hurt worse than almost anything she could remember.

She loved him and had for so very long, but she had come to realize that sometimes, love alone simply isn't enough.

They had been through so much together, all the ups and downs that life can throw at you ...

So, her heart was heavy and conflicted.

It whispered to hold on ... keep trying,

But she was too far gone.

The joy of their love had long since faded, and she couldn't even remember why they were fighting to stay together ...

It was the fights she remembered all too well.

His mean words and spiteful actions in the heat of the moment had taken a toll on her, and she finally admitted the truth she had resisted for too long:

She wasn't happy anymore, and no amount of communication, effort and date nights could mend her heart that he had torn apart, piece by piece.

She knew he would never understand and that he would blame her with cold words and even hateful names … but she was resolute.

She'd always love him, but she was going to find her own way now, without him.

She couldn't fix him, save him or change him – and she shouldn't have to try to …

She knew it wouldn't be easy, she'd miss him, and it would hurt, but it was more important for her to be happy than to stay in a relationship that was more misery than joy.

It's scary to take the first steps alone when you haven't been by yourself in such a long time …

But there was a sense of relief in her choice to step away.

Her heart, though conflicted, began to feel lighter … she noticed the feeling of a burden beginning to be lifted …

And that's when it all changed.

Her soul started to find the happiness again, and her sense of self appreciation began to return.

It would be a long and arduous road, but she was finally ready.

Maybe she'd stumble a time or two and maybe even shed a few tears along the way ...

But she was finally free to love herself and choose what mattered most every day:

Herself and her happiness.

She'd been through the rain, now it was time for her rainbow ...

And she couldn't help but smile.

She deserved everything ... starting with her new self ...

Beautiful, strong and free.

An Old Perfume, an Old Song, an Old Memory

I made a wrong turn, and suddenly some familiar sights greeted me that I hadn't seen in ages ...

Including one that I'll never forget.

Our favorite restaurant, where we met and made so many great memories.

I pulled over and felt a mixture of emotions as the past came rushing back –

Things I hadn't thought about for the longest time.

It's funny how something can trigger such an outpouring of emotion, whether it's a song, a place or even a smell ...

It takes you back to another time when you were a different person.

A smile crept across my lips as I thought of the joy that I experienced in that restaurant, with you.

It's been long enough now that the pain of us doesn't sting or haunt me like it used to, and I'm able to appreciate the beauty of what we had instead of drowning in the ugliness of the end.

I wonder what you're doing now, and I hope you're happy.

I wouldn't change a thing about what happened because I'm happier now than I've ever been.

What I learned about myself when we split up made me stronger and wiser, so I'm in a good place.

It doesn't mean that I don't miss you a little at random times like this, but you're right where you're supposed to be:

In my heart, not my life.

Some would say it's sad that we didn't work out, but I would respond that we were never meant to be.

I learned so much about myself and about love that I'm a better person for having gone through it.

I'll always cherish the happy memories and smile.

For a time, it was beautiful, it was us and it was love.

A Stranger Where Once There Was a Soulmate

I can't help but cry when I look at you now, wondering where we went wrong ...

Hurting as I try to understand.

It's hard when someone who was once so close slowly becomes a stranger.

I don't know where we lost our way or how we fell apart, but little pieces of my heart shattered every time we drifted further away from each other.

There was a time when our connection was powerful, and your love was so strong that I thought nothing could ever tear us asunder.

I couldn't have been more wrong, and now I just don't know what to do with these feelings of loss ...

I don't know what emotion to feel first:

Regret, sadness, anger ... so many visceral emotions wash over me about us.

As we have slowly stopped being close, it feels as though I have lost a little part of myself along the way.

I can't pick a time or place that caused us to become strangers, but I cry when I don't see the person I once knew behind your eyes.

This may be the hardest thing I've ever had to face, and the worst part is that I'm dealing with it alone.

I used to know everything you were thinking and all your heart's desires from just a single glance … and now, nothing.

I once held your heart in my hands and your soul whispered to mine every day …

But it's been so long since I've heard your soul that I don't think I even know you anymore.

I can't say if it's because you chose to hide from me, you don't care, or something happened …

I may never know.

I don't know if love can die, but I know some feelings can slowly fade away … and it's so heartbreaking that our love has dissipated into so very little … almost an apathy that tears my heart in two.

I wish I had the answers or knew what to do to fix us, but my heart tells me it's too far gone … you're too far away now.

How did we ever go from lovers to strangers?

Where did you lose your love for me and why?

As I close my eyes and try to hold onto the memories of the good times, I exhale forcibly and fight to hold myself together ...

And it takes every ounce of strength I have not to break down into tears.

Everything that's fallen apart – us, what's happened – it all just makes me sad.

Maybe we will find our way back to each other, but I can't hope for that any longer ...

I can't live trying to pin my heart onto dreams and maybes anymore.

I have to stay in those places where I can hold onto happiness, because memories are all that I have left of us now.

Maybe your soul will find mine once again in the darkness, but for now, that's just a fading dream and one that seems so far away.

I don't know what tomorrow will bring, but I can't think about the future right now.

I will live fully in the moments, find the beauty where I can and appreciate what I have.

It's sad that my happy thoughts come from the past now, but sooner or later, I'll have to move on.

I only hope and pray that you remember what we had before it's too late.

Either way, I'm doing what I have to do to be happy again … with or without you.

Today, I'm going to start living for myself again.

I'm taking back my magic, my life and my happiness …

One day,

One smile,

And one dream at a time.

Love and Pain: If One Can Fade, So Can the Other

She knew that he was wrong for her from the very beginning – bad boys usually are – but it didn't stop her from getting sucked into his world.

His passion and ferocity overwhelmed her senses in a way she'd never known because he wasn't like the others ...

In some intoxicating and dangerous ways,

But deep down, she knew the truth.

He wasn't going to be tied down, and she'd be chasing a ghost ...

So, she did the only thing she could and let him go.

It was one of the hardest things she'd ever had to do, but she knew it was necessary if she wanted to salvage the self-respect she had left.

It had been a whirlwind romance, a combination of desire and passion that swept her off her feet.

She tried to tell herself it was fleeting – just an affair, excitement from something different and new ...

But her heart whispered that it was more.

She shook her head defiantly.

It didn't matter what she wanted to believe, she had to fight her heart and listen to her judgement ...

A woman's intuition is rarely wrong.

She craved him in a way that was wholly unfamiliar to her, but she knew she needed to walk away and let him go ...

Before she got too deep.

It would be one of the hardest things she had ever done, but she was resolute and strong.

Exhaling fiercely, she gritted her teeth and decided to move on.

He would chase her, she knew, but for all the wrong reasons ...

And she needed someone to chase her for all the right reasons.

She knew that everyone comes into your life for a reason, a season or a lifetime, and she was thankful they had crossed paths.

He had shown her what true passion was and now, she wouldn't settle for anything less.

As she started her car and slumped back in the seat, tears came streaming down her face.

She'd miss him, she knew, but these would the last tears she would shed for him.

She needed and deserved more – he was unapologetically who he was and part of her loved him for it.

She was incredibly attracted to his fierce passion and alpha presence ...

But she was a complex woman who also needed soul, love and depth.

She shook her head.

When your heart wages against your head – when what you think you opposes what you know is best – that's the hardest fight of all.

But, if love can fade, then so can pain.

She drove away and she never looked back.

She moved on and evolved.

Smiling, she wiped the tears from her eyes.

She knew it would get harder before it would get easier, but she was strong enough to see it through.

And she knew she would come out better and stronger for it.

Because while he had shown her true passion, he would never be able to give her everything she truly needed,

And she deserved to be happy ... in all of the ways she wanted without exception or compromise ...
Now and for always.

Sometimes Doing What's Right Is the Hardest Choice

I look at my phone as your name pops up, and I sigh deeply.

It's a hard place to be when you know what you must do but your heart isn't totally ready to let go.

My mind has been screaming at me to move on for some time, a little bit louder with each fight or sleepless night.

I know what's best for me, and I have for some time, but love is a hard thing to ignore and just walk away from … that's where I'm stuck.

I gave us my all – being there through all the hard times and standing strong through the bad days – but sometimes, I felt like I was standing alone.

I tried to talk to you, share with you how I felt so that we could work through our problems and get back to loving each other the way we could ...

But you never really wanted to talk, you'd always say you were too busy or made me feel like it didn't matter to you.

Well, it mattered to me.

We mattered to me.

I guess I was the only one who felt that way.

You've broken my heart a little more every day with your apathy and hurtful words.

It's sad, but I've just hit that wall where my heart can't take any more.

I've got to take my happiness out of your hands because you've not really cared about that for a while ... and that's what hurts worst of all.

I just needed something – anything – from you to keep fighting for us, but I guess that was asking for too much.

Shame on you for making me believe that you wanted a future with me when we were fresh and new, and shame on me for holding on when you weren't even willing to put in the work.

It takes two people working together for a successful relationship, and that's something I don't know that you'll ever understand ... or maybe you just don't even care.

It really doesn't matter anymore.

My self-respect and self love are all I have left, and I'm done fighting for us ... I'm fighting for me now instead.

Maybe I'll look back one day with regret, but it will only be with the wish that things had gone differently and that you had met me halfway ...

That you had tried to make us work.

I did what I could do, and I'll move on knowing that I gave us our all.

Some people were meant to stay in our hearts, not in our lives.

I wish you the best, I'll never forget the time we had and the love we shared, but I've grown from this and learned more about myself ...

It won't be easy, and I'll still think about you from time to time,

But as I decide not to answer your call, I'm making the choice to move on and focus on me.

I'm working on loving myself more now.

What's meant to be will always find a way, so I know I'll end up where I'm supposed to be.

Wherever that is, at least I'll be happy again.

That, for now, will have to be enough.

Happy, free and at peace ... finally.

I Didn't Quit, I Simply Chose Myself

I know you think that I just gave up on us, but that's so far from the truth.

I didn't quit trying to love you, because I will always love you,

But sometimes love isn't enough … it takes effort too.

I quit trying to make it work with you because you weren't willing to do what it took for us both to be happy – not just you.

I tried to compromise, meet you halfway and do my part … but it takes two people to try, to put in the work for a relationship to be successful …

And you aren't willing to do what it takes.

So, no, I'm not choosing to give up on us,

I'm choosing myself and my own happiness over someone who says they care but then doesn't back it up with action.

I'm done believing the empty words.

I've cried so many tears and endured so many sleepless nights wanting you to just do something … anything.

I just wanted you to try.

I'm done chasing you, begging you to communicate and hoping that you'll show me that I'm worth the effort.

Sadly, you've shown me how much I don't really mean to you because if I did, you would do whatever it takes to help us make it through this ...

But you're not, and I don't think you ever will.

Maybe someone else would be okay with being an afterthought, but I'm not that person.

I deserve the best and I'm willing to work for it.

Someday, maybe, you'll find someone that you're willing to sacrifice for, but I doubt it.

That takes too much work.

So, before you spew angry words at me and blame me for quitting, take a good long look in the mirror.

I'll always love you and wish you the best, but I'm done fighting for someone who won't fight for us.

I'm going to start chasing my dreams and happiness instead ... and the thought makes me smile.

Maybe you'll realize what we had once I'm gone, but that's not my concern anymore.

I'm finally done … I'm all out of tears.
I choose me.
Maybe I won't be happy quickly, but I'll get there.
I deserve it. I'm worth it.
I'm more than enough.
One day, someone else may see that, but I'll be fine if they don't.
I don't need anyone else to tell me how amazing I am.
I know just how awesome I am because I believe in myself in a way you never did.
My future starts with me …
Today.
Thank you for setting me free.
Now I can finally fly again.
Strong, proud and free.

Are You Aching for Me Too?

I look over at the clock, and it's well past midnight … and I can't even begin to sleep.

The eerie silence of the house clings to me like a cloak, weighing me down with the heavy air of solitude.

My eyes are drawn to the other side of the bed where you would once lie beside me, peacefully dreaming.

The emptiness drives me to the point of tears as the feelings of missing you wash over me.

Since you've gone, nothing is the same.

I expect to hear your voice greeting me as I come home, and yet there's no sound.

I look at my phone as if your name will pop up and … nothing.

I try to dig down and hold onto the happy thoughts, but that gets harder and harder with each passing day.

My life is different now without you in it, and I've struggled to make peace with that.

Some days are harder than others, and I can't help but cry myself to sleep sometimes.

But as more time passes, it seems to get a little easier.

Maybe I'm just more accustomed to being alone or being without you, I don't really know.

I look over at where you used to lie beside me, and my heart still aches for you.

My mind races and wonders if you think of me too …

Do you long for me as I do for you?

I know I have to start finding my joy and letting you go, but it's so hard.

My friends try to help and encourage me, but I just don't know who I am without you anymore.

I tell my heart every day that what's meant to be will always find a way …

If you stay gone forever, then we were never written in the stars as I'd always dreamed.

It's hard to lose the one thing you thought would always be there – you, me … us.

As I roll over and clutch a pillow where I'd once be holding you, I bury my face and cry …

For us. For you. For what we lost somehow.

I know I'll feel better as the first rays of sunlight brighten my eyes, but right now I let my grief wash over me.

I know I'll look back and realize this was the way it had to be for me to reclaim my strength.

That doesn't make it any easier or hurt any less.

For now, I'll hold onto the happy memories, positive thoughts and know that this, too, shall pass.

I'll find my way back to myself and my happiness, but I know I'll shed more tears before I'm there.

I know the aching for you will slowly go away, but it still hurts, the longing does.

I don't know when or how, but I'll get past this.

Sometimes, you make a few detours on the way to your forever.

I guess you were always meant to be one of mine ... and I'm okay with that.

I'll be fine ... because I always am.

That's just what makes me beautiful –

All this brokenness I'm working my way through ...

I'm strong, I'm a fighter and I always find my way ...

One day at a time ... that's all I can manage right now.

It may not be pretty, it may not be easy,
But at least I'll always do it my way.

The Peace I Have Now Is Worth Everything

When I lost you, I thought I'd never be happy again.

For so long, you were all I could think of, and every happy thought or memory was tied to you.

I buried the pain from what happened between us and tried to distance my heart so that I could try to stop hurting, eventually ...

And truthfully, I really didn't know if the anguish would ever subside.

It seemed that all I could focus on was losing you and the sadness that caused ...

But when I began looking for hope, something miraculous happened ...

I found myself instead.

All the things I had lost in us, all the parts of me that vanished as I tried to make you happy ... they slowly started to reappear.

I had spent so much time chasing you or vying for your attention that I had stopped doing the things that made my soul happy.

Incredibly, every day that passed ... I rediscovered a little more of myself.

With those remembered pieces, the pain began to subside slowly ... a bit more each day ...

Until finally, the hurt was much like you – a distant memory of a time and a feeling that couldn't hurt me anymore.

When you walked away from me, I thought I had lost everything, and the funny thing is, just the opposite happened.

I found it all instead – everything that mattered and that I had needed all along:

My happiness, my peace and most of all, my love for myself.

You gave me the greatest gift of all by letting me go ... you pointed the way back to me.

And now, I'm never looking back.

I've got no interest in living in the past and revisiting the pain ... there's nothing there for me now.

I found a love in my heart and a peace in my soul ... and it was because of me, not you.

It's strange, really, that the end of our relationship wasn't really the end at all.

It was the beginning of everything good that I needed to find again.

I had been lost for too long, but not anymore.

I'm on my way back home now.

Thank goodness for the broken roads that led me to exactly where I was always meant to be.

My Silence Means I'm Finally Done

I gave you everything I had … heart, mind, body and soul.

It still wasn't good enough.

You made me feel horrible about myself in so many ways every day for reasons that didn't even matter.

The worst part was that you justified every mean thing you did and all the cruel words that you spewed at me …

Saying you were just trying to help me get better.

Get better at feeling worse about myself?

We fought so many times because you had to have the last word, you were always right … or so you thought.

I don't know when we stopped loving and started fighting for our survival as a couple, but it doesn't matter anymore.

I'm sure you'd have an answer and would blame it on me if you could ...

But I'm not asking you, because you've pushed me so far that I'm not crying anymore.

I'm just numb now.

Numb to your words, your promises and your apologies.

I have nothing left to give. I've spent everything I had trying to save a relationship that I'm not even sure you care about …

Or at least that you don't care about as much as you do yourself.

There're so many things that I'll never understand … but I don't have to.

I've run out of words, feelings and the energy to try to care about you anymore.

It's time now to put myself first, something I haven't done in a long time … that stops now.

Don't get me wrong, I hope the best for you, sincerely.

Just not as a part of my life.

I'm hard enough on myself without you adding to the onslaught.

So, as you're wondering why I'm not calling you back and not fighting with you on text anymore, the reason is very simple … and powerful.

I'm done.

No more chances or trying to work things out.

I'm walking away, lifting my head up and trying to find the light again.

I know I've got a hard road ahead of me and I'll probably miss you a lot, but truthfully,

I miss me more.

I miss the old me, loving, beautiful and strong ... the woman who could do anything and was always finding the happiness in her life.

I don't blame you for anything – I take responsibility for every time I allowed you to treat me badly and all the ways that I didn't stand up for myself.

That's also why I'm taking responsibility for my life back and walking away.

I'm owning my choices and my happiness,

Finally, after spending way too long allowing myself to feel like a victim,

Because I'm not.

I'm closing this chapter of my life and starting anew.

I don't know where I'm going or how I'll get there, but as I say goodbye to a past filled with anguish, I'm starting to finally feel the sunlight again.

Now, it's my time to get my shine back.

It's my time again ...
To rise again, to fly high and most of all,
To just be happy.

Sometimes the Purest Forum of "I Love You" is "Goodbye"

I know you'll never forgive me for walking away from us, and that's okay, I'll have to live with that.

You've kept pushing me to fight for us, to hold on.

You said you thought we could make it work.

But that's just it ... we have been down that road so many times before, and it never worked, not even a little.

We both tried with all our hearts and did all we could do, but together, you and I were toxic.

We were magical in the very beginning – butterflies and passion catapulted our hearts to heightened sensations of love, desire and need – but somewhere along the way, we lost ourselves and each other, and it all turned dark.

There wasn't just one event or a single act, but a gradual turn, and slowly I felt bad and then worse.

I'm done trying to figure out what went wrong or how to fix us, because we are way past that now.

So, before we end up hating each other, I'm letting you go.

Not because I don't love you or that it's easy, it's just what my heart tells me is right.

We've tried everything, and I can't fight any more for something that I know isn't meant to be ... we are just oil and water, which tears my heart in two.

I hope, over time, you'll forgive me for loving you enough to let you go ...

It won't be easy for me either, but I know it's the right thing to do.

I know we won't be happy for a while as we lead newly separate lives, but we haven't been happy together for a while.

You'll blame me, hate me and make me the bad guy, and I'll have to live with that.

As I write these words with tears in my eyes, I know that some say that real strength lies in holding on ...

I now know that letting go is the hardest thing I'll ever have to do.

Maybe one day, you'll think of me and smile, but if you don't, that's okay, too.

I'm doing what I think is right for us both to be happy ...

Maybe we'll meet each other in the next life and things might be different.

Until then, I'll miss you and wish you the best.

I'm taking my own road, and it'll be hard.

But I'll be fine ... I always am.

I know somehow and someday I'll end up exactly where I'm meant to be, and so will you.

I'm not saying goodbye ... I'm saying I love you enough to let you go.

I hope one day you'll understand.

When You Didn't Fight for Me

I thought you would always be the one I could count on who would stand up for me when things got tough.

I'd always believed you would fight for me because of how you felt about me.

Turns out, I was wrong.

While I know we had some rough times of late, our relationship had a lot of truly beautiful moments too ...

Or had you forgotten those, too?

When I needed you most, when things were the hardest ... you just turned your back on me.

I don't think I've ever been so hurt in my life.

I just couldn't believe the one person that I thought would always be there ... wasn't.

You just chose to walk away rather than fight for me, for us?

I ask myself a million questions trying to understand how you could do that ... and honestly, I don't know.

I may never know.

Maybe you didn't feel as strongly about me as you claimed, maybe something changed ... or maybe you just fed me some words to make me believe we were the real thing.

I don't know. I'm just so hurt – I'm beyond pain, I'm numb.

I don't know where to turn or what to think, I'm completely lost.

This wasn't supposed to be how things were meant to turnout.

Part of me always believed you were the one and that my search was over ...

And now I'm just feeling dumb as you left me holding pieces of my broken heart.

But when everything came crashing down around me, you were nowhere to be found ...

So, I did what I never thought I could do and stood up for myself.

I fought for me when I didn't even think I had that kind of strength.

Sometimes, your story doesn't give you a choice, and that's exactly where you walked out on me ...

So, I did whatever I had to do to survive.

It's hard, I'm not going to lie – there are so many days when I want to quit – but I'd rather be out here struggling by myself than depending on someone who walks out when things get hard.

I'm done with that.

I'm sure you have your reasons and excuses, but you never even bothered to explain it to me ... the one person you should have told first, you didn't even think I was worth the effort.

I guess it's better to find out now than many years down the road, but it still hurts all the same.

I know I'll be fine eventually, because your cowardice showed me a strength I didn't know I had.

I'm strong enough, brave enough and courageous enough to pull through this with my head held high.

You walked out when the going got tough, but the toughness just made me get going.

I guess I should thank you for showing me the way back home to myself, but I don't know that I'll ever forgive you for what you did to me.

Doesn't really matter because I'm in a better place now.

Where you left a girl to fend for herself without a thought to how she'd make it,

There now stands a strong woman ...
With a heart of gold and a fiery spirit.
Some warriors are born ...
This one was forged in the fire.
I was made for this ...
Strong, beautiful and finally free.

If It Wasn't Love, Then It Was a Lesson

I thought it had it all figured out until you came into my life.

You said everything I wanted to hear, did all the right things and swept me off my feet.

It seemed too good to be true, but I wanted so much to believe in you and love ... that I did.

A whirlwind romance had me floating ... until the parts of our love story started to unravel.

The magic stopped and the butterflies went away and soon I was left fighting for a relationship so unhappy that I didn't even know what I was fighting for anymore.

I tried to see past the fights, the anger and the disrespect, but it just became too hard.

I realized I was fighting for my happiness, and it didn't feel good anymore – none of it.

Heart in pieces, I walked away carrying what I had left of my self-respect and dignity ...

Crying every step of the way.

You acted as though you cared and told me all the ways we'd be better, but I soon learned actions speak louder than words ... for your actions never changed.

I tossed and turned in bed trying to analyze what went wrong, if it was my fault and what I could have done differently ...

And all that did was cause more pain and bring back more hurtful memories.

I did what I had to do to survive – I moved on.

You made it a battle every step of the way, and I've had to do the things I thought I would never have to do ... disappear to you altogether, because "goodbye" wasn't an answer you were willing to accept.

I'm done being scared and looking out the window, wondering if you're going to show up.

That's not living.

I'm putting the past – and us – behind me, and I'm not going back there.

I'm looking forward to the future ... I'm going to be happy again someday, somehow.

Maybe it won't be tomorrow or next week, but I'll get there.

Maybe it was love in its own way, I'll never know for sure, but I learned so much from our time that I'm growing into a stronger, wiser and better me because of it.

Some come into your life for a season, a reason or a lesson, and you were all three.

You've shown me what I want – and don't want – in love, and I know now that I'll never settle for less.

I've stopped dwelling on what went wrong, and I'm learning instead.

It's a painful lesson, but it'll make me better for it.

I'm turning the page and starting a new chapter of my life.

This one I'm calling simply ...

"Happiness."

The Hardest Part of Waking Up

I woke up, hoping to feel refreshed after a night spent tossing and turning.

It was one of those long nights when I couldn't turn off my thoughts and my memories wouldn't give me a moment's peace.

So, as I opened my eyes, I mustered every bit of optimism about the start of a beautiful day ...

Until my heart whispered the lingering thoughts I had wanted to forget.

You. Us.

The pain of our split was all too real and felt like just yesterday, though it had actually been a couple weeks already.

I knew that no matter what I told myself or what I wanted, my heart wasn't ready to let you go ...

Even though my head kept telling me to move on.

That's one of the hardest places to be – where your head is at war with your heart.

Deep down, I knew what was best for me and what I needed to do, but there was no convincing my heart of that reality.

My emotions weren't there yet, so I was stuck, all the time, between a mind trying to forget and a heart that wouldn't let me.

It was a constant montage at night, playing a never-ending stream of us – good, bad and ugly ...

But always us.

I did the best I could and just fought for a few hours' sleep, if that, in between the nonstop thinking.

Though, as I sipped my coffee one morning, I noticed that everything hurt just a little less and the sunlight was a little bit brighter.

Maybe, I thought, this is how it happens.

The more time passes, the less you feel, the less you hurt, the less you remember ...

Until one day, it's all just a distant memory.

I couldn't help but smile at the possibility of relief.

I knew I'd have to make peace with the past before I could ever really move on, but suddenly, I felt a twinge that I hadn't before.

Maybe it wasn't a bold epiphany and maybe it didn't make anything better instantly ... but now, I finally realized that I could do this.

Things would get better; the pain would begin to subside; I'd start to find my way again.

That, for now, would have to be enough.

After all, now, I had something I didn't have last night, and it changed everything ...

Something that had been eluding me for far too long ...

Hope.

And I decided to keep building on that ... all the way to my newfound happiness.

It might take a while, but I finally knew that I could make my way away from the pain of us.

Step by step and day by day, I'd start to love myself again ...

And finally, be able to let you go.

I Would Rather Be Alone Than Have a Love That Is Lonely

I tried … I really did.

I poured everything I had into us, in every way I knew how to try and keep our love alive.

What I learned the hard way is that it takes two people to make a relationship truly work.

I won't blame you for your choices because you did what made you happy – and obviously, my happiness wasn't part of that agenda.

I gave you everything and asked for so little in return, and that was my first mistake.

I sacrificed, gave and loved all that I could, but I should have demanded more.

I deserve more.

By lowering my expectations, I lost self-respect and started losing myself, too.

It's a lonely feeling to be in a relationship and not have anyone you can talk to or confide in …

But that's where we've ended up, and I'm done settling for less than what I'm worth.

It's no one's fault but my own for allowing things to end up in this place.

Maybe if I'd stood up for what I wanted and truly needed, things might have been different ... I'll probably never know.

What I do know is that walking away now with some shred of my dignity and self-respect means more than waiting around on someone who doesn't really seem to care.

I've told you all this time and again, and like always, you'd brush me off and tell me I was being needy ...

And yes, I did need you to step up and show me that you loved me, not just say the words you thought I wanted to hear with no action to back them up.

I never thought love could make me feel empty, alone and isolated, but that's just where I am.

Really, though, it's not love making me feel that way – it's the lack of love.

So, as I leave my key and a note on the table, know that I'll always care about you, but sometimes, that's just not enough.

I'm doing what I need to do to be happy again, and if you care even a little, you'll let me go in peace to find my way.

After all, I know I'll be better off on my own than having an empty and lonely love story ... because we both know that's not really a love story, it's just a story.

But thanks to you, I know everything I don't want in another person or a relationship.

I'm taking this time for me now, and it's long overdue.

Love isn't going anywhere, and I'm done trying to turn projects into partners.

I'm choosing the love story where I know I'll get what I give ...

I'm loving myself first now.

And there's nothing wrong with that if you ask me.

One step at a time, finding my way back to the light.

I can do this.

No Turning Back

She lay in bed crying, caught in the middle of that hard battle between heart and mind.

He had made his choice and did so in the worst possible way.

He didn't come to her and talk to her about how he felt ... he sought the arms of another.

She had loved him for so long and finding out that way shook her to her core.

She was a confused mess of anger and sadness ... she had no words for the way she felt at that moment.

She wanted to scream at him, unleash the overwhelming rage she felt for his deceitful choice ... but she knew that would do no good.

He had tried to apologize, told her all the things he thought she wanted to hear ... but she wasn't the type of woman who tolerated infidelity.

There was nothing he could say or do that would change her mind about what she knew she had to do ...

But her heart – the one part of her that wouldn't let her close the door fully – still loved him, wanted to believe in him, and longed to give him another chance.

Deep down, she knew she had no choice but to let him go ...

But that didn't make letting go any easier.

She caught herself looking at old pictures of them together, transporting her back to a happier time – when their love was young, and the future seemed limitless.

Wiping away a tear, fighting to pull herself together, she picked up her phone and typed out a message.

Finishing the text and pressing send, she was overwhelmed with a combination of relief and sadness ...

Actually, much more than that, but those were the emotions that struck her first.

Her heart pounded and she fought to catch her breath as she stared at the message she had just sent to him.

She was doing what she knew had to be done, but it didn't make it any easier.

With those few words, she had made her choice.

What she sent him was more than just a message for him, it was a statement to herself that she was closing this chapter of her life.

If she talked to him again, she feared she would give in.

She still cared about him, and the wounds were too fresh ...

Her heart wasn't ready to let go.

So, she sent him a message that gave her the start to a new path ...

Which scared and excited her at the same time ... "I'm done ..."

Now, with a few simple words, she was free.

It would be a hard few weeks and months ahead, but with determination, courage and healing ...

She'd be happier, eventually.

Looking forward to better days made a slight smile creep over her face.

That, for now, would have to be enough.

Free to find her own way ...

Back to the light.

Back to herself and happiness.

Love Me from the Inside Out

When he left, he broke her ...

Or so he thought.

Truth was, at the time, she thought the same thing.

Shattered into countless pieces, she tried to pick them up by moving on.

She lost herself in him because he made it seem safe and so easy ...

Only it wasn't so safe and the easy just disappeared with a single phrase.

"It's over."

He thought he wanted something different, believed she wasn't good enough for him,

he thought he was the one who deserved better.

He didn't know what he wanted, and she paid the price for that.

He couldn't have been more wrong about who she was and the strength she had.

She had lost her sense of self and who she was meant to be ...

She stopped living her life and started living his, for him.

But that all changed on a stormy Saturday that she cried so many times about.

He did her a favor by setting her free, pushing her away because he never really understood the beauty of her soul and unconditional love.

He opened her eyes to who she was and what she wanted.

She wasn't an object, a toy or a hobby.

The love she had known wasn't really love at all – it was bending to his needs in his way without getting the respect she needed.

Their love wasn't a love at all ... and it definitely wasn't a two-way street.

She decided that she'd rather be soul food than eye candy.

Her journey now wasn't about becoming anything; it was about unbecoming everything that wasn't really her – and never was.

She'd rather be loved for her scars and flaws than admired for fake perfection.

Beautiful chaos instead of blatantly boring,

She knew that she deserved so much more ...

She wanted the truth, no matter how harsh, instead of the lies that had once soothed her.

She realized that true beauty isn't about a pretty face and a nice figure,

It's the depth of your soul and love in your heart.

The most beautiful makeup for a woman isn't found in a store …

It's the passion in her heart, depth of her character and the allure of her soul.

She didn't just survive the fire,

She became more than a candle in the wind –

She roared like a damned wildfire.

He wanted arm candy without a voice and beauty without soul.

Luckily for her, his mistake was her blessing.

He woke her up to the gorgeous possibilities that lay before and within herself.

Beauty without depth is just window decor.

With all her mysterious scratches and disastrous dents, she desired to be loved for who she truly was.

She finally realized that she wanted to be loved from the inside out.

I Won't Lose Who I Am to Become What You Want

When you decided I wasn't the one for you anymore, you helped me realize a few things about myself that I guess I never knew.

Sure, I'd been battered, bruised and broken and thought I'd lost my way completely, but I hoped I always had you in my corner.

Turns out, you weren't in this for me after all.

Truth is, I had started to lose who I was trying to make you happy.

They say sometimes love just isn't enough ...

This is one of those times.

You wanted me to be what you wanted, on your terms, in your way.

In your mind, you had this picture of who and what you thought I should be ...

Your happiness mattered more than mine, and it always would.

I thought I could change to make you happy, but I lost myself in the process.

Did you ever really love me for me?

Or was it just what I embodied and what I represented?

Did you ever really see me for who I am?

When you saw that I was strong enough to stand up for who I was and wouldn't give into your selfish requests ...

You decided that you'd had enough.

Getting what you wanted meant more than supporting and loving me in the way I deserved – for who I truly was.

Now that I'm walking out of your life, I can't help but cry inside.

Cry for what I thought we had.

Cry for what we could have been.

Cry for the love that I wish was real.

Maybe you loved me in your own way, hoping that I would change to be everything you wanted me to be ...

But that's just it.

Love is acceptance.

Love is understanding.

Love is true.

Asking me to change who I am to be what you want isn't love at all.

I'm just glad I saw the truth before I lost myself trying to please you.

I'll never forget the times we had and the smiles we shared, but you gave me the greatest gift of all, and I'm thankful for that reason.

You showed me that I'm good enough to be loved on my terms for all my flaws and uniqueness.

Nothing and no one will ever change my self-worth because I won't let that happen.

My jagged edges and imperfect flaws are just the things that make me beautiful.

You didn't appreciate that about me, but someone will,

That's where I'll find my happily ever after.

Loving another imperfect person perfectly.

Some people were meant to be in your heart, not your life.

I'm holding out for the one who deserves to be in both.

The Greatest Gift

He walked away, stealing away so many of my hopes and dreams in an instant.

Truthfully, it was my fault for giving him that power, but I'd always been the one to follow my heart, and I fell in love hard when I did.

As he left, I realized that losing myself in what was once "us" had destroyed everything I thought I had been.

The days and nights seemed to run together as my heart bled the pain of broken dreams and lost love.

I'd lost myself in what he wanted me to be, and in the end, he had cast me aside without care.

I didn't hear his words as he tore apart my heart, only the bleeding emotions that were sinking my soul.

When the one thing you believe will always be forever vanishes into yesterday, it shakes your foundations to the very core.

Somewhere along your spiral to the depths of discontent, you lose everything that you once believed to be true about yourself.

You stop believing the good things and begin to hear only the negativity that slowly seeps into your soul.

The bad is always easier to believe than the good ... especially when you've lost yourself and your heart has shattered into countless pieces.

But that's the thing about being broken: the light slowly begins to permeate the cracks of your broken soul ... if only you let it.

Piece by piece, I forged the fires that once consumed me into lighting my new path.

I didn't always know where I was going or even how I was going to get there, but as time passed, I became more determined on my journey back to a better me ... a happier place.

Losing yourself means that you have the chance to rise from the ashes, stronger than ever before ... to create a stronger self.

I took the small acts of self love along the way and began to finally understand who I was meant to be all along.

In the end, he gave me the greatest gift possible by turning his back on me ...

His choice led me to the path that breathed life into a brighter and better future ahead.

I turned my wounds into wisdom and my setback into a comeback.

I no longer accepted less than I deserved, and I finally realized my worth.

I was worthy of the best – from myself and everyone in my life.

And I learned the most important truth of all:

Strong people aren't born, they're forged by the fires they walk through.

I turned my can'ts into cans and my dreams into plans.

Rise or shine, I'll always give what I get, and I have a lot of love to share.

I'll never let my past define me, and I'll always let my passion breathe life into my dreams.

Most of all, I realized the most wonderful gift of all: I don't have to be perfect ...

I just have to be me.

My story will always be a tale with failures, crashes and loss ...

But more than that,

It'll be about rising again and shining brightly.

I'm strong, I'm worth it,

And I'll always be more than enough.

I Never Blamed You … I Only Blamed Me for Making You My Everything

When I think about what happened to us, it just makes me sad.

Not because of what you did, but because of what I let myself become …

I stopped being myself and started trying to be something I wasn't … to make you happy.

I lost myself in us so much that there wasn't a "me" anymore – at least not the person that I used to be.

That's not your fault, it's mine.

You didn't ask me to change but part of you hoped I would become what you wanted.

You thought you would be happy if I changed … and it still wasn't enough to save us.

We lost our way and learned that sometimes, love alone just isn't enough.

I don't know all the reasons why we didn't work, only that I never should have pinned all my hopes and happiness on you.

That wasn't fair to you, and it never gave us a chance.

I thought I was doing what you wanted, being what you needed to be happy ...

But I was wrong.

Who I became and what happened made both of us lose faith in ourselves and each other.

I've found the strength to forgive you for walking away,

But more than that, I uncovered the courage to forgive myself.

Most of all, I should thank you for setting me free to make my way back to start my journey of self-discovery.

I was so lost for so long because I depended on you to make me happy, and when you left, I didn't think I would ever be whole again.

So many days, I didn't even want to get out of bed, because wallowing in misery seemed so much easier than digging myself out of the sadness.

That's when something clicked in me, and I realized I needed to remember who I was ... before you, before us, before the heartbreak.

Strong, beautiful and vibrant, I was once a wonderful soul who loved my life.

The path back to myself hasn't been easy, and there have been days I wanted to quit, but I found my way, somehow.

I'll never forget us and the times we had; it'll always have a special place in my heart.

But it no longer defines me, and it no longer hurts ...

That's how I know I've healed and made peace with all that happened.

Thank you for showing me the way back home to myself.

I know now that I'm loved, I'm special and I'm worthy ...

Of all the love in the world.

I finally remembered how to love myself the way I should have all along.

Exactly Why It Had to Happen

I sit here in the dark, fighting back the tears while I'm lost in the thoughts and memories of what we once had.

The pain … it can hurt so much that it makes all else seem not to matter.

How can something you wanted so much not work out the way you'd always hoped?

I loved you with all my heart, gave our relationship everything, but still, I'm alone trying to hold it together … and failing.

Tears flow down my cheeks as the images of us cascade across my mind …

Memories of what we had make me smile … and cry.

Yes, there were amazing moments, but there were also angry fights and hurtful words.

There's so much I wish I could take back and change, but we can't undo the damage that's been done.

I try to tell myself that we will still work out, that we will find a way, but deep down, I know this is goodbye.

I don't know where we went wrong or exactly why we fell apart, because there was so much love there …

But sometimes, love just isn't enough.

Things started slipping through my fingers as we grew apart and every disagreement caused our hearts to become a little more bitter.

I close my eyes and I just try to stop the thoughts, the memories, the pain … but I can't.

Everything is too fresh and too real.

I never knew emotional pain could feel so physical and so intense, until now.

It's in these moments, at our lowest, that we approach the crossroads.

I was standing there, in my overwhelming grief, not knowing what to do or how I would make it through this ...

When a bleep from my phone drew my attention.

I wiped my eyes and tried to see through my tear-stained vision.

Words from one of my oldest and dearest friends.

"If it wasn't meant to be, nothing you can do will change that … don't spend so long staring at a lost past that you forget how to embrace a beautiful future of possibility."

I smiled and shook my head at those wise words.

Sometimes, when you're at your lowest, you will see a sign … it was up to me to take it to heart.

But she was right. I was so focused on the why of what happened that I would never make peace with it until I let it go.

I had to accept it so my heart could begin to heal.

I may never know the why or how, only that it did.

I'd never see the new doors opening if I kept staring at the closed door of us.

I closed my eyes, inhaled deeply and made myself a promise I would remind myself of every single day.

What's meant to be will always find a way, and my future and happiness is all in my hands.

If it's meant to be, it's up to me.

I'm letting go of the past to make room for what may be ...

I don't know what tomorrow will bring, but I know for reasons I can't explain, that someday, I will look back and know exactly why it had to happen.

And I will smile, because my broken road led me right to where I always needed to be.

You Are Strong Enough to Start Again

Yes,

You are strong enough to survive this.

I know it seems like your world is over and maybe you can't find the light right now, but hang in there.

I know your soul is weary and you feel like you can't keep going, but don't stop.

Your happiness may seem so far away, but it's not as far as you might think.

Yes, the nights can be long, and you don't have the answers,

But you don't have to.

Breathe.

Take a moment and remember what all you've survived before now.

You've been through the fire and always found your way … your courage has been forged in the fires that tried to take you down.

Remember that – you're a warrior who will continue to rise again.

It's time to find your magic and listen to your heart.

It knows the way, but you've gotten so weary that you've lost sight of the path.

If you've lost faith in yourself and your strength is waning, know that you're not alone.

You're loved, you're enough, and I believe in you.

It's always darkest before the dawn, and this is your time to start again.

Every end is a new beginning, and your next chapter will be magical ...

You just have to start believing in yourself like I believe in you.

Like all the people in your life do.

I know you're reading this and wondering how you'll make it through, but I'm telling you ... You've got this.

You are meant for more than to simply fizzle out like a dampened flicker of light.

You're a wildfire capable of setting your soul and life on fire again.

Take my hand and let's start climbing out of the darkness, day by day.

I know you've been looking for a sign, something to believe in ...

Well, this is it.

Today is your wake-up call, and this is where you start again – you're strong enough and you're worth it.

It won't be easy, and it won't be fast, but it will change your life if you're ready.

These words were meant for you.

Are you ready to start again?

Believe, Darling … in you, your destiny and most of all, in that you are meant for more.

Beginning today … get up, step up and start remembering the magic and dreams you lost along the way.

Anything's possible if you just believe …

And I believe in you.

Burning Bridges:
The Breakup Playbook

Find more love, hope and empowerment at
www.houseofravenwolf.com
including Ravenwolf's complete works
and quote merchandise.

Anything's possible if you just believe ... and I believe in you.

www.ingramcontent.com/pod-product-compliance
Ingram Content Group UK Ltd.
Pitfield, Milton Keynes, MK11 3LW, UK
UKHW042001230426
12048UKWH00009B/468